Be.
I Am.

HOW TO LIVE GOD'S PURPOSE FOR
YOUR LIFE TODAY

Joseph Zorzoli

TRILOGY CHRISTIAN PUBLISHERS
TUSTIN, CA

Trilogy Christian Publishers
A Wholly Owned Subsidiary of Trinity Broadcasting Network
2442 Michelle Drive
Tustin, CA 92780

All scripture quotations are taken from the Authorized King James Version of the Bible unless otherwise noted. Public domain.

For information, address Trilogy Christian Publishing

Rights Department, 2442 Michelle Drive, Tustin, Ca 92780.

Trilogy Christian Publishing/ TBN and colophon are trademarks of Trinity Broadcasting Network.

For information about special discounts for bulk purchases, please contact Trilogy Christian Publishing.

Manufactured in the United States of America

Trilogy Disclaimer: The views and content expressed in this book are those of the author and may not necessarily reflect the views and doctrine of Trilogy Christian Publishing or the Trinity Broadcasting Network.

10 9 8 7 6 5 4 3 2 1

Library of Congress Cataloging-in-Publication Data is available.

ISBN 978-1-63769-214-1

ISBN 978-1-63769-215-8 (ebook)

Contents

John 3:17

For **God** did **not** send **His Son** into the world to **condemn** the **world**, but that the world through **Him** might be **saved**.

(New King James Version)

John 19:30

So when **Jesus** had received the sour wine, He said, **"It is finished!"** And bowing His head, He gave up His spirit.

(New King James Version)

Romans 8:39

nor **height** nor **depth**, nor any other **created thing**, shall be able to **separate us** from the **love** of **God** which is in **Christ Jesus our Lord**.

(New King James Version)

2 Corinthians 5:17

Therefore, if **anyone** is in **Christ**, he is a **new creation**; old things have passed away; behold, all things have become **new**.

(New King James Version)

1 John 4:17

Love has been perfected among us in this: that we may have boldness in the day of judgment; because as **He is, so are we in this world**

(New King James Version)

How to Live God's Purpose for Your Life Today

The objectives of this writing are the following:

- Establish basic truths about the Word of God.
- Reveal God's purpose for your life on this Earth.
- Reveal who you are according to God, your Creator.
- Examine the pitfalls that prevent you from living God's purpose on this earth.
- Give you specific instruction to overcome those obstacles and avoid the pitfalls that exist in this world.
- Reveal how you will operate in the world as you live God's purpose and how your world will look and respond as you do so.
- Give you a practical guide on how to get started *today*.

Before we began this journey together, it is critical to understand that what you are about to read deals with issues of the spirit. As farfetched or foolish as it may seem to some folks, the message is all based on spiritual truths from the eternal Word of God. This reasoning is not mine but that of the Holy Spirit. I absolutely believe and value the message. It continues to change the way I see the world and operate in it, and I know it will do the same for you. All I ask is for you to keep an open mind and an open heart as you learn the powerful truth about living God's purpose for your life today.

1 Cor 2:12-15

12 We have not received the spirit of the world but the Spirit who is from God, that we may understand what God has freely given us. 13 This is what we speak, not in words taught us by human wisdom but in words taught by the Spirit, expressing spiritual truths in spiritual words. 14 The man without the Spirit does not accept the things that come from the Spirit of God, for they are foolishness to him, and he cannot understand them, because they are spiritually discerned. 15 The spiritual man makes judgments about all things, but he himself is not subject to any man's judgment.

(New International Version)

Hear God's Word + Think God's Word + Know God's Word + Believe God's Word + Speak God's Word = Be God's Word

Establish Basic Truths about the Word of God

We have a choice according to the Bible: 1) We can either believe the Word of God, which is life, the invisible, established in the beginning and will remain true for eternity, or 2) We can believe in the things of the world, which are death, the visible and most importantly, are temporary.

- **Deut 30:19**

  This day I call heaven and earth as witnesses against you that I have set before you life and death, blessings and curses. Now choose life, so that you and your children may live.

  (New International Version)

- **Heb 11:3**

  It is by faith that we understand that the universe was created by God's word, so that what can be seen was made out of what cannot be seen.

  (TEV)

- The Word is God. God is the Word.
- Jesus is the Word of God made flesh.
- The Word of God is the everlasting Truth.
- It takes faith to believe in the Word of God.

  - John 1:1
    In the beginning was the Word, and the Word was with God, and the Word was God. 2 He was with God in the beginning.

  - Luke 21:33
    Heaven and earth will disappear, but my words will remain forever.

  - Heb 4:12
    For the word of God is living and active. Sharper than any double-edged sword, it penetrates even to dividing soul and spirit, joints and marrow; it judges the thoughts and attitudes of the heart.

  - Isa 46:9
    Remember the former things, those of long ago;
    I am God, and there is no other;
    I am God, and there is none like me.

  - Isa 55:11
    So shall My word be that goes forth from My mouth;
    It shall not return to Me void,

But it shall accomplish what I please,
And it shall prosper in the thing for which I sent it.

Basic Truths about God:

God is The Word; the Word is God.

- John 1:1
  In the beginning was the Word, and the Word was with God, and the Word was God. 2 He was with God in the beginning.
  (New International Version)

God is Life.

- John 6:48
  I am the bread of life.
  (New International Version)

God is Truth.

- John 14:6
  Jesus answered, "I am the way and the truth and the life. No one comes to the Father except through me."
  (New International Version)

God is light.

- 1 John 1:5
  This is the message we have heard from him and declare to you: God is light; in him there is no darkness at all.
  (New International Version)

God is spirit.

- John 4:24

  "God is spirit, and his worshipers must worship in spirit and in truth."

  (New International Version)

God is love.

- 1 John 4:8

  Whoever does not love does not know God, because God is love.

  (New International Version)

God is good.

- I Chronicles 16:34

  O give thanks to the LORD; for he is good; for his mercy endures for ever.

  (American King James Version)

God is Creator of heaven and earth.

- Gen 1:1

  In the beginning God created the heavens and the earth.

  (New International Version)

God is our Creator.

- Gen 1:27

  So God created man in his own image,
  in the image of God he created him;
  male and female he created them.

  (New International Version)

God is omnipresent/omnipotent

- Isa 46:9-10

  9 Remember the former things, those of long ago;
  I am God, and there is no other;
  I am God, and there is none like me.
  10 I make known the end from the beginning,
  from ancient times, what is still to come.
  I say: My purpose will stand,
  and I will do all that I please.

  (New International Version)

Hear Truth + Think Truth + Know Truth + Believe Truth + Speak Truth = Be Truth

Reveal God's Purpose for Your Life on This Earth

God's purpose for your life is for you to be the truth. Not for you to try to be the truth. Just be truth. To think truth, talk truth, walk truth, live truth effortlessly. After all, God says we are created in his image; therefore, we are what God is! The last time I checked, he is the Truth, the Way, and the Life!

- **Gen 1:27**

  So God created man in his own image,
  in the image of God he created him;
  male and female he created them.

  (New International Version)

- **1 John 4:16-17**

  We have come to know and have believed the love which God has for us. God is love, and the one who abides in love abides in God, and God abides in him. 17 By this, love is perfected with us, so that we may have confidence in the day of judgment; because as He is [right NOW], so also are we in this world.

- Anything contrary to the Word of God is a lie because God does not lie!

  - Rom 3:4
    God forbid: yea, let God be found true, but every man a liar; as it is written, That thou mightest be justified in thy words, And mightest prevail when thou comest into judgment.

    (American Standard Version)

The Matrix – The World in which We Live

- I define the "world" as is the world we live in, the world we wake up to, the world we are so intricately connected to, and a world of "belief systems" that are a complicated, contradictory, cluttered matrix of human consciousness.

- I equate this matrix (the world's belief systems) to the tree of knowledge of good and evil in the Garden of Eden.

- Gen 2:16-17

  And the LORD God commanded the man, saying, "Of every tree of the garden you may freely eat; 17 but of the tree of the knowledge of good and evil you shall not eat, for in the day that you eat of it you shall surely die."

  (New King James Version)

- We have all been eating from that tree of knowledge of good and evil ever since.

- The adage "you are what you eat" applies in the spirit realm as well. Be careful what you are feeding your spirit. It's a matter of life and death.

- There is without question truth in the world in which we live. We must, as spirits of God, be able to discern the truth from the lies.

- The world's belief systems are oftentimes contrary to the Word of God, the truth. Therefore many things the world holds as truth are not because they are contrary to the Word of God, God's truth.

- The world we live and trust as our reality is based on lies and deception; therefore, we must trust in what God's Word says over what we see in the world.

- The Devil has created this "matrix," and this "matrix" does not align with God's truth.

- Just consider some of the things people believe in and live by and even die for.

- For example:

    - Some people believe if they are a martyr for their religion, they will have 72 dark-eyed virgins who will live with them on the other side.
    - Some people believe bathing in cow urine protects them from evil spirits.
    - Some people believe a large amount of money will bring peace to their lives and solve all their problems. Some people believe if they could get a certain person to love them, they would finally have peace.
    - Some people believe if they could get married and start a family, life would be full of peace and joy.
    - Some people believe if they could get that promotion at work, all would be right with their world.
    - Some people believe if they could be famous, or prettier, or skinnier, or younger, life would finally come with peace, joy, and happiness.

- These are all lies in and of the world. Many of us have been fooled to believe in one lie or another.
- We can even look at religions and countries to see the lies they believe.

- o Many Middle Eastern groups believe if they can get rid of the Jewish people in the region, they can finally be at peace.
- o Some groups in the Darfur region believe if they can cleanse the region of rival ethnic tribes, their people can have peace.

- These are real-life examples of the kind of lies people believe, and some are willing to die for!
- Bottom line: Good people can believe bad things, too. Things that do not align with God's truth.

- o 2 Corinthians 4:4
  The god of this age (Satan) has blinded the minds of unbelievers, so that they cannot see the light of the gospel of the glory of Christ, who is the image of God.
  (New International Version)

Hear God's Word + Think God's Word + Know God's Word + Believe God's Word + Speak God's Word = Be God's Word

Reveal Who You Really Are According to God, Your Creator

Let your thoughts be God's thoughts. Even though we live in the world, we are not of the world, so let our thoughts and words be based on the Word of God and not based on the belief systems of the world. That is why it is so critical to know the Word of God; because the Word of God is what God says is so. If you do not know the Word of God, you'll never be able to discern between what is truth (those things that line up with the Word of God) and the lies and deceptions of the world (those things that do not line up with the Word of God).

- **John 17:15-18**

  15"My prayer is not that you take them out of the world but that you protect them from the evil one. 16They are not of the world, even as I am not of it. 17Sanctifyb them by the truth; your word is truth. 18As you sent me into the

world, I have sent them into the world. 19For them I sanctify myself, that they too may be truly sanctified"
(New International Version)

- **Hosea 4:6**
  My people are destroyed for lack of knowledge.
  (New International Version)

- **2 Corinthians 2:10**
  I don't want Satan to outwit us. After all, we are not ignorant about Satan's scheming.
  (God's Word Translation)

- **1 Peter 5:8**
  Be self-controlled and alert. Your enemy the devil prowls around like a roaring lion looking for someone to devour.
  (New International Version)

The BIG LIE

- The most detrimental lie we are told is about ourselves.
- At one point or another, we all are guilty of living and believing in those things that do not line up with who God says we are based on the blood of Jesus.

- We all are born in this world and soon thereafter start calling ourselves firemen, presidents, plumbers, bus drivers, executives, movie stars, kings, football players, basketball players, CEOs, dishwashers, generals, doctors, lobbyists, lawyers, pharmacists, nurses. Still, the truth is these are things we do, but not who we are, for we are much greater.

- Take the case of the man who was born to a peasant family long ago. He was told all his life that he was a peasant and would never be much more than that.
    - He agreed with the lies about who he was and lived his life as a defeated man.
    - Much like us, he was his own worst enemy at times, agreeing with the lies and piling on by calling himself much worse than those things said about him by others.
    - At the end of his life, he found out that he was a direct descendent of the king and royalty since birth!
    - The defeated man had been living a life based on lies and deception, for he had the blue blood of royalty flowing through his veins.

- Do you think had he known he was a direct descendant of the king that his life would have been different?

- Do you think he would have had the same internal conversations with himself had he known he was royalty since birth?
- Do you think people would have treated and talked to him the same way had they known he was a child of the king?

  - Prov 23:7

    For as he thinks in his heart, so is he.

    (New King James Version)

- This is a true story.

- One major difference: the story is not about some random man long ago who muddled through life as a defeated man, not knowing who he was, but a story about you, a story about me.
- Our story ends differently, though, because we are embarking on a new day learning about who we really are in Christ Jesus.

- You will begin your journey anew, armed with basic truths about who you are in, and through, Christ Jesus.

- You are a child of the most-high God.
  - Romans 8:16

The Spirit Himself testifies with our spirit that we are children of God.

(New American Standard)

- You are a New Creation.
  - 2 Cor 5:17-19

    17 Therefore, if anyone is in Christ, he is a new creation; the old has gone, the new has come! 18 All this is from God, who reconciled us to himself through Christ and gave us the ministry of reconciliation: 19 that God was reconciling the world to himself in Christ, not counting men's sins against them.

    (New International Version)

- You are a spirit created in the image of God.
  - Gen 1:27

    So God created man in his own image,
    in the image of God he created him;
    male and female he created them.

    (New International Version)

- You are loved and adored by God Almighty.
  - John 3:16-17

16 "For God so loved the world that he gave his one and only Son, that whoever believes in him shall not perish but have eternal life. 17 For God did not send his Son into the world to condemn the world, but to save the world through him."

(New International Version)

- You are a son of God.
  - o Gal 3:26-27

    26 You are all sons of God through faith in Christ Jesus, 27 for all of you who were baptized into Christ have clothed yourselves with Christ.

    (New International Version)

- So anything thing less than this is contrary to what God says about you.
- Your life and others will benefit as you grow in the ways of God.
- That is the powerful truth.

- Therefore the hunger we are all trying to fill and the thirst we are all trying to quench can only be filled and quenched with spiritual things from your Creator.
- Nothing else will work!
  - o John 6:35

Then Jesus declared, "I am the bread of life. He who comes to me will never go hungry, and he who believes in me will never be thirsty."

(New International Version)

Hear God's Word + Think God's Word + Know God's Word + Believe God's Word + Speak God's Word = Be God's Word

Examine the Pitfalls that Prevent You from Living God's Purpose on This Earth

Behaving badly causes many of us to run from the cross, to run from God. God wants us to do something that seems to be a bit counterintuitive, especially when we behave badly. He wants us to run to the cross, not from the cross. After all, was not that the point of the Cross? Did Jesus not die on the Cross to save us from our sins? When we are behaving badly, and we don't run to the Cross, we're not benefiting from the grace of God, the grace that He has so freely given us and paid an enormous price to do so, through his Son, Jesus Christ. Jesus said he did not come for the healthy but the sick. It indeed takes faith to believe in God's mercy and grace. It takes faith to believe in the powerful and redeeming blood of the lamb, Jesus Christ. Yes, without a doubt, our behavior is often contrary to who God says we are in Christ Jesus. I get that. But I say to you, even when our actions do not line up with who God says we are, we must continue to stand in faith and believe in who God says we are. We must believe in God's mercy and grace and that the blood of Jesus is more than enough to cover all of our sins: past, present, and future. I believe my God is not a liar: He proclaims that his Son. Jesus, who died on the cross to eradicate my sins, is more than enough. Therefore I believe Jesus is more than enough! More than you or I will ever need! All of this other stuff in the natural will eventually work its way out through the Holy Spirit. Just believe.

- **Matthew 9:11-12**

  11When the Pharisees saw this, they asked his disciples, "Why does your teacher eat with tax collectors and 'sinners'?" 12On hearing this, Jesus said, "It is not the healthy who need a doctor, but the sick. 13But go and learn what this means: 'I desire mercy, not sacrifice.' For I have not come to call the righteous, but sinners."

  (New International Version)

- **Romans 3:23**

  For all have sinned and fall short of the glory of God

  (New International Version)

- **Heb 11:1-3**
  To have faith is to be sure of the things we hope for, to be certain of the things we cannot see. 2 It was by their faith that people of ancient times won God's approval. 3 It is by faith that we understand that the universe was created by God's word, so that what can be seen was made out of what cannot be seen.

  (TEV)

Why it takes faith

- So what gives? God says it is impossible to please Him without faith: seeing those things that are not as though they were.

  - Heb 11:6
    And without faith it is impossible to please God, because anyone who comes to him must believe that he exists, and that he rewards those who earnestly seek him.

    (New International Version)

- No wonder it is impossible to please God without faith.
- It takes faith to believe in God and what He says about you rather than the feedback the world so

gladly gives regarding who you are and what value you bring to this world.

- After all, how can you grow close to God and walk in his presence if you believe what the world says to be so?
- If you're wondering, you can't.

    - Matthew 17:20
      He replied, "Because you have so little faith. I tell you the truth, if you have faith as small as a mustard seed, you can say to this mountain, 'Move from here to there' and it will move. Nothing will be impossible for you."
      (New International Version)

Hear Truth + Think Truth + Know Truth + Believe Truth + Speak Truth = Be Truth

Why we behave so badly:

- **Gal 5:17-18**
  17For the sinful nature desires what is contrary to the Spirit, and the Spirit what is contrary to the sinful nature. 18They are in conflict with each other, so that you do not do what you want.
  (New International Version)

- **Mark 7:21-23**
  21 For from within, out of the heart of men, proceed evil thoughts, adulteries, fornications, murders, 22 thefts, covetousness, wickedness, deceit, lewdness, an evil eye, blasphemy, pride, foolishness. 23 All these evil things come from within and defile a man."
  (New King James Version)

- The Good News is God knows what shape we're all in, and he sent his Son, Jesus Christ, to clean up our mess.

  - Rom 3:22-25
    22 This righteousness from God comes through faith in Jesus Christ to all who believe. There is no difference, 23 for all have sinned and fall short of the glory of God, 24 and are justified freely by his grace through the redemption that came by Christ Jesus. 25 God presented him as a sacrifice of atonement, through faith in his blood.
    (New International Version)

- Do not believe the lies of the world.
- Do not believe what the devil is saying about you or your brothers and sisters in Christ. Believe what God says about you and His body. Not necessarily how the body is behaving.

- What you see with your natural eyes, God sees with His eyes, which are spiritual for He is Spirit, or should we say eyes peering through the wisdom, knowledge, and understanding of His Word: the eyes of God.
- It is important to keep in mind that we are talking about our natural existence in a spiritual context, which makes this a bit tricky to explain, but it is the most critical truth you can grab onto and understand.

  - John 6:27

    Life is spiritual. Your physical existence doesn't contribute to that life. The words that I have spoken to you are spiritual

    (God's Word translation)

- I am suggesting that we take a step back and look at our life from a different perspective, through our spiritual eyes. I'm not suggesting that when we are behaving badly that we pretend we are not.
- You must understand it's not your behavior, good or bad, that aligns you to who God says you are, but it is your faith, the spiritual stuff.
- Faith, meaning it is you choosing to believe that you are righteous, without sin, because of Jesus dying on the cross for your sins even though you active-

ly engage in sin. That is what I mean when I say it takes faith. "Faith is the substance of things hoped for, the evidence of things not seen" (Hebrews 11:1).

- Your righteousness, or your spiritual perfection, is not based on your works or lack of works; your deeds or lack of deeds; your acting right or not acting right, but it is based on the blood of Jesus. God's Grace: God sending his Son, Jesus, to the earth, to die for our sins. All we have to do is believe. Why is it so hard to believe?
- Our righteousness is truly an undeserved gift from God. By His grace, we have been saved through faith in Jesus Christ. These things are of the Spirit, spiritual truths, spiritual stuff, God's Word, which must be discerned by the spirit within you.

  - Eph 2:1-10

    In the past you were spiritually dead because of your disobedience and sins. 2 At that time you followed the world's evil way; you obeyed the ruler of the spiritual powers in space, the spirit who now controls the people who disobey God. 3 Actually all of us were like them and lived according to our natural desires, doing whatever suited the wishes of our own bodies and minds. In our natural condition we, like everyone else, were destined to suffer God's anger. 4 But God's mercy is so abundant, and his love for us is so great, 5 that while we were spiritually dead in our disobedience, he brought us to life with Christ. It is by God's grace that you have been saved. 6 In our union with Christ Jesus he raised us up with him to rule with him in the heavenly world. 7 He did this to demonstrate for all time to come the extraordinary greatness of his grace in the love he showed us in Christ Jesus. 8 For it is by God's grace that you have been saved through faith. It is not the result of your own efforts, but God's gift, so that no one can boast about it. 10 God has made us what we are, and in our union with Christ Jesus he has created us for a life of good deeds, which he has already prepared for us to do.

(TEV)

Hear God's Word + Think God's Word + Know God's Word + Believe God's Word + Speak God's Word = Be God's Word

Be aware of the schemer.

- **2 Corinthians 2:10**

  I don't want Satan to outwit us. After all, we are not ignorant about Satan's scheming.

  (God's Word Translation)

- **1 Peter 5:8**
  Be self-controlled and alert. Your enemy the devil prowls around like a roaring lion looking for someone to devour.
  (New International Version)

- The enemy says some pretty mean things about all of us in very sneaky ways.
- We are bombarded every day by messages from television shows, music videos, movies, commercials, magazines, radio, music, religions, people, etc.
- The enemy uses these messages to shape our thoughts about who we are and how we rank against the world's benchmarks.
- All of these lies lead to what you think and believe about the world, yourself, and how you as a person stack up to all this nonsense.
- Hence, your inward thoughts align with the lies of the world and are manifested in how you view the world and yourself in it.

  - Prov 23:7
    For as he thinks in his heart, so is he.
    (New King James Version)

- These thoughts are detrimental in pursuing God's truth about who you really are in Christ.

- Below are some kind of inward thoughts that we often contribute to this collective calamity of human consciences we call the world.

- These are examples of the world's messages with which we all are bombarded with every day:
    - You are a loser.
    - You are a failure.
    - You are undeserving.
    - You are a miserable person.
    - You are full of anxiety.
    - You are full of depression.
    - You are lacking confidence.
    - You are undisciplined.
    - You are a bad person.
    - You are unlovable.
    - You are a drunk.
    - You are a drug addict.
    - You are ugly.
    - You are a quitter.
    - You are hateful.
    - You are lonely.
    - You are dumb.
    - You are worthless.
    - You are nothing.
    - You are joyless.
    - You are a sinner.
    - You are the opposite of God. Just face it.

- Enough already, we get the message, and every day we get the message loud and clear.

- Scary stuff when you plug it into "hear, think, know, believe, speak = be."

  - Prov 23:7
    For as he thinks in his heart, so is he.
    (New King James Version)

- Of course, these are all lies because these things do not align with what God says about us!

  - Gal 3:26-27
    26 You are all sons of God through faith in Christ Jesus, 27 for all of you who were baptized into Christ have clothed yourselves with Christ.
    (New International Version)

Hear Truth + Think Truth + Know Truth + Believe Truth + Speak Truth = Be Truth

<u>God is your Father:</u>

- Is it not amazing to think that God, the Creator of the universe, created you in his image and calls you son or daughter? Just think, God Almighty, your heavenly Father, loves you so much He sent His Son Jesus to die on the cross for your sins so that you may be saved, born again, and perfect in His eyes! I suggest you stop and really think about it, soak it in for the next few hours, days, weeks, years, and try to wrap your brain around such an amazing truth. How is it that we can feel so lonely, rejected, devalued when we are who God says we are? We are children of God, royalty who are universally recognized. Let's start acting like it!

- You are alive because of God, your Father, the one and only God!
    - 1 Cor 8:6

      Yet for us there is but one God, the Father, from whom all things came and for whom we live; and there is but one Lord, Jesus Christ, through whom all things came and through whom we live.

      (New International Version)

- You are created in the image of God!
    - Gen 1:27-28

      So God created man in His own image; in the image of God He created him; male and female He created them.

      (NKJV)

- You are a child of the most-high God!
    - Romans 8:16
      The Spirit Himself testifies with our spirit that we are children of God.
      (New American Standard)

- God says to choose what He says about you, not what the world says.

- In other words, choose to believe the truth, not lies.

- You have the power to choose who to believe.

- You can choose to believe what the devil says about you or what God says about you.

- God says choose life, not death!

    - Deut 30:19-20
      19 This day I call heaven and earth as witnesses against you that I have set before you life and death, blessings and curses. Now choose life, so that you and your children may live 20 and that you may love the LORD your God, listen to his voice, and hold fast to him. For the LORD is your life, and he will give you many years in the land he swore to give to your fathers, Abraham, Isaac and Jacob.
      (New International Version)

Hear God's Word + Think God's Word + Know God's Word + Believe God's Word + Speak God's Word = Be God's Word

So who does God say you are?

- You are more than a conqueror, and you are loved by God!
    - Rom 8:37-39

      37 No, in all these things we are more than conquerors through him who loved us. 38 For I am convinced that neither death nor life, neither angels nor demons, neither the present nor the future, nor any powers, 39 neither height nor depth, nor anything else in all creation, will be able to separate us from the love of God that is in Christ Jesus our Lord.

      (New International Version)

- You are the head, and not the tail, in Christ Jesus!
    - Deut 28:13-14

      13 "The LORD will make you the head and not the tail, and you only will be above, and you will not be underneath, if you listen to the commandments of the LORD your God, which I charge you today, to observe them carefully, 14 and do not turn aside from any of the words which I command you today, to the right or to the left, to go after other gods to serve them.

    (NASU)

- You are strong, courageous, and disciplined!
    - 2 Tim 1:7

      For God has not given us a spirit of fear and timidity, but of power, love, and self-discipline.

      (NLT)

- You are a new creation in Christ Jesus!
    - 2 Cor 5:17-19

      17 Therefore, if anyone is in Christ, he is a new creation; the old has gone, the new has come! 18 All this is from God, who reconciled us to himself through Christ and gave us the ministry of reconciliation: 19 that God was reconciling the world to himself in Christ, not counting men's sins against them.

      (New International Version)

- You are a son of God!
    - Gal 3:26-27

      26 You are all sons of God through faith in Christ Jesus, 27 for all of you who were baptized into Christ have clothed yourselves with Christ.

      (New International Version)

- You are righteous in Christ Jesus!
    - Rom 3:22-24

      22 This righteousness from God comes through faith in Jesus Christ to all who believe. There is no differ-

ence, 23 for all have sinned and fall short of the glory of God, 24 and are justified freely by his grace through the redemption that came by Christ Jesus.

(New International Version)

- You can do anything through Christ Jesus!
  - Matt 19:26

    Jesus looked at them and said, "With man this is impossible, but with God all things are possible."

    (New International Version)

Hear God's Word + Think God's Word + Know God's Word + Believe God's Word + Speak God's Word = Be God's Word

The Big Lie:

- We live in a physical world, for all intents and purposes, the only world we have ever known, which, by the way, has been based on lies. We, too, live in a spiritual world, the invisible, the world in which God operates, where truth is living and active.

  - Col 1:15-16

    15 He is the image of the invisible God, the firstborn over all creation. 16 For by him all things were created: things in heaven and on earth, visible and invis-

ible, whether thrones or powers or rulers or authorities; all things were created by him and for him.
(New International Version)

- Heb 11:1-3
  To have faith is to be sure of the things we hope for, to be certain of the things we cannot see. 2 It was by their faith that people of ancient times won God's approval. 3 It is by faith that we understand that the universe was created by God's word, so that what can be seen was made out of what cannot be seen.
  (TEV)

- Heb 4:12
  For the word of God is living and active. Sharper than any double-edged sword, it penetrates even to dividing soul and spirit, joints and marrow; it judges the thoughts and attitudes of the heart

- One of the most critical lies the world tells us is that the world we live in can bring us peace, joy, and happiness.
- But there is a catch: it must come through human pursuits because, after all, we are all human.

- The human pursuit of peace, joy, and happiness comes in many forms. It is usually determined or influenced by the messages we buy into and are bombarded with every day by the physical world (the Matrix):

- o Money
- o Material possessions (cars, houses, boats, etc.)
- o Youthful appearances
- o Fame
- o Sex
- o Power/Clout
- o Relationships
- o Religion

- These things temporarily satisfy the human condition but will not ultimately give us peace, joy, and happiness.

- The world's offerings cannot satisfy our spirit man because our spirit man can only be satisfied by spiritual offerings, which are God's truth about who we are and our purpose on earth.

  - o 1 Cor 2:12-15

    12 We have not received the spirit of the world but the Spirit who is from God, that we may understand what God has freely given us. 13 This is what we speak, not in words taught us by human wisdom but in words taught by the Spirit, expressing spiritual truths in spiritual words. 14 The man without the Spirit does not accept the things that come from the Spirit of God, for they are foolishness to him, and he cannot understand them, because they are spiritually discerned. 15 The spiritual man makes judgments about all things, but he himself is not subject to any man's judgment.

(New International Version)

- John 6:27
  Life is spiritual. Your physical existence doesn't contribute to that life. The words that I have spoken to you are spiritual

  (God's Word translation)

- The only thing the physical world can offer us is sinful pleasures and empty promises that satisfy only for a season.
  - Heb 11:25
    He chose to share the oppression of God's people instead of enjoying the fleeting pleasures of sin.

    (New Living Translation)

- So what does the human pursuit of happiness look and sound like?
  - If only I could win the lottery...
  - If only I could get that promotion...

- If only I could be famous...
- If only I could make the A-list...
- If only I could date this girl...
- If only I could get rid of that girl...
- If only I could have done this in life instead of that...
- If only I could afford that house...
- If only I could start my own business...
- If only I could find a man...
- If only I could have a baby...
- If only I could get another hit...
- If only I could make some new friends...
- If only I could move out of this neighborhood...
- If only I could sin less...
- If only I could break this addiction...
- If only I could have a family...
- If only I could mend my broken family...
- If only I could have more help around the house...
- If only I could lose some weight or get plastic surgery...
- If only I could find a peeing cow...

- I think we have all been guilty of believing at least some of this nonsense at one time or another in our lives.
- I am not suggesting that you don't have or need goals in life.

- All I am saying, should you reach your worldly goals, be prepared for the realization that it will not satisfy your deepest yearnings of spiritual fulfillment. It will not bring lasting happiness to your natural existence or peace and joy your spirit man truly longs for.

- In fact, knowing that your current goal attainment will not bring you lasting happiness, peace, and joy, you may decide to reevaluate what it is you are pursuing in life: who or what you are seeking first.

- King Solomon, the wisest man who ever lived, gives his take on what the world has to offer:
    - o Eccl 2:1-11

      I thought in my heart, "Come now, I will test you with pleasure to find out what is good." But that also proved to be meaningless. 2 "Laughter," I said, "is foolish. And what does pleasure accomplish?" 3 I tried cheering myself with wine, and embracing folly—my mind still guiding me with wisdom. I wanted to see what was worthwhile for men to do under heaven during the few days of their lives.4 I undertook great projects: I built houses for myself and planted vineyards. 5 I made gardens and parks and planted all kinds of fruit trees in them. 6 I made reservoirs to

> *water groves of flourishing trees. 7 I bought male and female slaves and had other slaves who were born in my house. I also owned more herds and flocks than anyone in Jerusalem before me. 8 I amassed silver and gold for myself, and the treasure of kings and provinces. I acquired men and women singers, and a harema as well—the delights of the heart of man. 9 I became greater by far than anyone in Jerusalem before me. In all this my wisdom stayed with me.10 I denied myself nothing my eyes desired;I refused my heart no pleasure. My heart took delight in all my work,and this was the reward for all my labor.11Yet when I surveyed all that my hands had done and what I had toiled to achieve, everything was meaningless, a chasing after the wind;nothing was gained under the sun.*
>
> (New International Version)

- The truth is we are spiritual beings first, who live in a human body to live in a physical world.
- The truth is that the pursuit or attainment of worldly things, whether in the days of King Solomon or today, will never bring you lasting peace, joy, or happiness.
- The truth is peace and joy can only come through things of the Spirit.

- o John 6:63

  "It is the Spirit who gives life; the flesh profits nothing; the words that I have spoken to you are spirit and are life."

  (New American Standard)

Hear Truth + Think Truth + Know Truth + Believe Truth + Speak Truth = Be Truth

You are a Spirit:

- **Zech 12:1**

  This is the word of the LORD concerning Israel. The LORD, who stretches out the heavens, who lays the foundation of the earth, and who forms the spirit of man within him, declares:

  (New International Version)

- Imagine if you were on the moon. Your spacesuit would be essential to living in that environment.
- Therefore, maintaining your spacesuit would be a necessary and worthwhile endeavor.
- The things you do to maintain the spacesuit are not the same things you'd do to maintain your body.
- What makes sense for the spacesuit does not necessarily make sense for your human body other than

needing the spacesuit to survive on the moon's surface.

- As your body still needs water, food, etc., to sustain life, your spacesuit has other needs such as mechanical, electrical, and hydraulics to maintain its functions.
- This holds true for your spirit man: things a human body requires, such as food, water, and shelter to sustain itself, do not apply to nourishing the spirit.
- The spirit requires things of the Spirit: spirit food from God.
- Spirit food is the Living Word of God. God's truth about you and your purpose as a child of God.

    o John 6:27
    "Do not work for food that spoils, but for food that endures to eternal life, which the Son of Man will give you. On him God the Father has placed his seal of approval."
    (New International Version)

Hear Christ + Think Christ + Know Christ + Believe Christ + Speak Christ = Be Christ-like

The Truth of the Matter:

- It is impossible to find peace and joy through worldly pursuits of ideas or things.

- You name it, and the truth is it will not bring you lasting happiness, peace, or joy: billions of dollars, fame, drugs, cars, boats, planes, relationships, clothes, beauty, youth, glamour, religion, cow urine: it doesn't matter. These things are all just a bunch of silly lies. Take the word of King Solomon, only the richest, wisest man who ever lived.

- Don't waste your time pursuing these things, for this is a fruitless endeavor.

- Most of the world will never reach such lofty goals or aspirations, and the ones that do typically wind up with another list to pursue and are never satisfied.

- This takes me back to rule #1: You are a spirit being, and the spirit can only be satisfied with spiritual things from God your Creator.

- Most religions set a mark that is impossible to hit by any human trying to wield their way to perfection. This can only be obtained through the law of the Spirit, which can only come by grace, through faith in Christ Jesus.

- Trying to achieve righteousness through one's own effort is an impossible and tormenting path to pursue. I believe it is insulting to God. What would be the point of the cross if we could do it on our own?

- Religion applies spiritual goals to the believer, which are impossible to achieve through the human flesh. That is the reason so many churches are riddled with hypocrisy.

    - Rom 7:14-25

      14 For we know that the law is spiritual, but I am carnal, sold under sin. 15 For what I am doing, I do not understand. For what I will to do, that I do not practice; but what I hate, that I do. 16 If, then, I do what I will not to do, I agree with the law that it is good. 17 But now, it is no longer I who do it, but sin that dwells in me. 18 For I know that in me (that is, in my flesh) nothing good dwells; for to will is present with me, but how to perform what is good I do not find. 19 For the good that I will to do, I do not do; but the evil I will not to do, that I practice. 20 Now if I do what I will not to do, it is no longer I who do it, but sin that dwells in me. 21 I find then a law, that evil is present with me, the one who wills to do good. 22 For I delight in the law of God according to the inward man. 23 But I see another law in my members, warring against the law of my mind, and bringing me into captivity to the law of sin which is in my members. 24 O wretched man that I am! Who will deliver me from this body of death? 25 I thank God -- through Jesus Christ our Lord!

(New King James Version)

- There are a few people whom we may have considered to have reached the pinnacle of success. The fact remains they still do not have peace of mind because of their worldly success.

- Remember rule #1.

    - John 6:27
      Life is spiritual. Your physical existence doesn't contribute to that life. The words that I have spoken to you are spiritual.

      (God's Word translation)

Hear Truth + Think Truth + Know Truth + Believe Truth + Speak Truth = Be Truth

Give You Specific Instruction to Overcome Those Obstacles and Avoid the Pitfalls that Exist in This World

The key is in the spirit realm! You are a spirit. The only way you, the spirit, can have peace and joy is through things of the Spirit. You, the spirit man, can only be satisfied by spiritual food: gifts of the Spirit. You, the spirit man, can only satisfy your spiritual appetite with spiritual food.

- **Rom 8:5**
  For they that are after the flesh do mind the things of the flesh; but they that are after the Spirit the things of the Spirit.

(King James Version)

- **Rom 14:17-18**
  17 For the kingdom of God is not a matter of eating and drinking, but of righteousness, peace and joy in the Holy Spirit, 18 because anyone who serves Christ in this way is pleasing to God and approved by men.
  (New International Version)

- **Galatians 5:22-25**
  22 But the fruit of the Spirit is love, joy, peace, patience, kindness, goodness, faithfulness, 23gentleness and self-control. Against such things there is no law. 24Those who belong to Christ Jesus have crucified the sinful nature with its passions and desires. 25Since we live by the Spirit, let us keep in step with the Spirit.
  (New International Version)

<u>What is spirit food? How can I feed my spirit?</u>

- Hearing and meditating on God's Word, the truth about who you are in Christ Jesus, is a fantastic example of spiritual food.

  - John 6:35-40
    35 Then Jesus declared, "I am the bread of life. He who comes to me will never go hungry, and he who believes in me will never be thirsty. 36 But as I told you, you have seen me and still you do not believe. 37 All that

the Father gives me will come to me, and whoever comes to me I will never drive away. 38 For I have come down from heaven not to do my will but to do the will of him who sent me. 39 And this is the will of him who sent me, that I shall lose none of all that he has given me, but raise them up at the last day. 40 For my Father's will is that everyone who looks to the Son and believes in him shall have eternal life, and I will raise him up at the last day."

(New International Version)

How to feed your spirit:

- Hear Truth + Think Truth + Know Truth + Believe Truth
- Hear God's Word + Think God's Word + Know God's Word + Believe God's Word
- Hear Christ + Think Christ + Know Christ + Believe Christ

Specific examples of spiritual food:

- You are more than a conqueror and loved by God!
  - Rom 8:37-39

    37 No, in all these things we are more than conquerors through him who loved us. 38 For I am convinced that neither death nor life, neither angels nor demons, neither the present nor the future, nor any powers, 39 neither height nor depth, nor anything else in all creation, will be able to separate us from the love of God that is in Christ Jesus our Lord.

(New International Version)

- You are the head and not the tail in Christ Jesus!
    - o Deut 28:13-14

      13 " The LORD will make you the head and not the tail, and you only will be above, and you will not be underneath, if you listen to the commandments of the LORD your God, which I charge you today, to observe them carefully, 14 and do not turn aside from any of the words which I command you today, to the right or to the left, to go after other gods to serve them.

      (NASU)

- You are courageous, strong and disciplined!
    - o 2 Tim 1:7

      For God has not given us a spirit of fear and timidity, but of power, love, and self-discipline.

      (NLT)

- You are a new creation in Christ Jesus!
    - o 2 Cor 5:17-19

      17 Therefore, if anyone is in Christ, he is a new creation; the old has gone, the new has come! 18 All this is from God, who reconciled us to himself through Christ and gave us the ministry of reconciliation: 19 that God was reconciling the world to himself in Christ, not counting men's sins against them.

(New International Version)

- You are perfect in Christ Jesus!
    - o Rom 3:22-24

      22 This righteousness from God comes through faith in Jesus Christ to all who believe. There is no difference, 23 for all have sinned and fall short of the glory of God, 24 and are justified freely by his grace through the redemption that came by Christ Jesus.

      (New International Version)

- You can do the impossible through Christ Jesus!
    - o Matt 19:26

      Jesus looked at them and said, "With man this is impossible, but with God all things are possible."

      (New International Version)

- You are truly loved by God, your Father!
    - o John 3:16-17

      16 For God so loved the world, that he gave his only begotten Son, that whosoever believeth in him should not perish, but have everlasting life.17 For God sent not his Son into the world to condemn the world; but that the world through him might be saved.

KJV (Scripture)

- You reside in Christ Jesus as Christ Jesus resides in the Father God!
  - o John 14:19-20

    19 Before long, the world will not see me anymore, but you will see me. Because I live, you also will live. 20 On that day you will realize that I am in my Father, and you are in me, and I am in you."

    (New International Version)

- Keep in mind when reading about God's truth, about who you are in Christ Jesus, that it is critical to apply God's truth in the correct context.

- Many people read God's word and immediately start applying these truths to the physical world they live in. They soon become discouraged because they do not see their physical world aligning with God's truth.

- In fact, their thoughts, beliefs, and words quickly start realigning with what they see in the world instead of God's Word. The visible and temporary versus the invisible and everlasting. They go back to their old way of thinking, believing, and talking, based on the feedback they receive from the world, and often not aligned to God's truth.

- o 1 Cor 2:12-15

  12 We have not received the spirit of the world but the Spirit who is from God, that we may understand what God has freely given us. 13 This is what we speak, not in words taught us by human wisdom but in words taught by the Spirit, expressing spiritual truths in spiritual words. 14 The man without the Spirit does not accept the things that come from the Spirit of God, for they are foolishness to him, and he cannot understand them, because they are spiritually discerned. 15 The spiritual man makes judgments about all things, but he himself is not subject to any man's judgment:

  (New International Version)

- They give up and go back to believing what they see in the world, which keeps them from living God's intended purpose for their lives. They say, "Life still sucks. It all sounded good, but more of the same old, same old for me!"

- This is because they chose to believe their "worldly reality" and not the Word of God, their "spiritual reality."

- These truths are spiritual truths and should be applied to the spiritual world, the realm where God exists, where His word is living and active.

- The good news is that the spiritual world always takes precedence over the natural world; Every time.

    - John 1:1-2
      In the beginning was the Word, and the Word was with God, and the Word was God. 2 He was with God in the beginning.
      (New International Version)

    - Heb 11:3
      It is by faith that we understand that the universe was created by God's word, so that what can be seen was made out of what cannot be seen.
      (TEV)

- It has to happen in the spirit world first before it is manifested in the physical world. Good or evil.

    - Gen 1:4
      In the beginning God created the heavens and the earth. 2 Now the earth was formless and empty, darkness was over the surface of the deep, and the Spirit

of God was hovering over the waters.3 And God said, "Let there be light," and there was light. 4 God saw that the light was good, and he separated the light from the darkness.

(New International Version)

- Do not look for changes in the natural realm as you begin to grow in the spirit of God, but look for changes in the spiritual realm instead.

- As things change in the spirit, these changes will begin to manifest in your physical world.

Hear God's Word + Think God's Word + Know God's Word + Believe God's Word + Speak God's Word = Be God's Word

Reveal How You Will Operate in the World as You Be the Truth, and How Your World Will Look and Respond as You Do.

If you think about it, God intended for things to be much different for all of us. I know this because God prepared a perfect world for Adam and Eve. There was no sickness, disease, death, poverty, hunger, etc.; the world God created was truly perfect in every way. This world without sin is made for us too! The original sin changed everything, though, which was Adam and Eve's disobedience to God. When Adam and Eve sinned against God, sin entered the earth and brought death and destruction with it. Before sin, the world was perfect as God intended it to be. The good news is that Jesus is the answer to the original sin, a do-over but much better. Although Adam and Eve only had been given one chance, God gives us all the chances we'll ever need because of His mercy and grace in His Son, Jesus Christ. Think about this: if sin is negated in our lives, as God says it is, this carries some amazing benefits for all of us. To break it down: those things that came into our world because of sin, such as sickness and diseases, all require sin to exist, as these things are the consequences of sin. So God negated sin in our lives; therefore, the consequences of sin are negated too! In other words, the consequences of sin, sickness and disease, no longer have a right or authority to exist in your life since God negated the very thing these things need to exist in our lives. One cannot exist without the other. It takes faith to believe what God says.

Now I am not suggesting the world around you will become perfect. We can't control those things around us, as people have free will and do, in fact, exercise that will to do some pretty evil things. But we do have the amazing power to choose to believe the eternal Word of God over the temporary craziness we see in the world. We can choose to believe in the blood of Christ that wipes away the sins of the world and the consequences that come with it. Imagine how God is perfect love, joy, and peace regardless of all the evil things happening in the world. God knows the things of this world are temporary, and His Word has the final say; it will not return to Him void, for His Word is eternal and true. God's love, peace, and joy are not affected in the least by the things of the world. The good news is that we, too, can have love, peace, and joy. Just like God, our love, peace, and joy do not have to be affected by the things of the world. The joy of the Lord is my strength! Just believe.

How God fixed the problem:

- **1 Peter 2: 21-24**
  For you have been called for this purpose, since Christ also suffered for you, leaving you an example for you to follow in His steps, 22 WHO COMMITTED NO SIN, NOR WAS ANY DECEIT FOUND IN HIS MOUTH; 23 and while being reviled, He did not revile in return; while suffering, He uttered no threats, but kept entrusting Himself to Him who judges righteously; 24 and He Himself bore our sins in His body on the cross, so that we might die to sin and live to righteousness; for by His wounds you were healed.

- **Isaiah 53:5**
  But he was pierced for our transgressions, he was crushed for our iniquities; the punishment that brought us peace was upon him, and by his wounds we are healed.
  (New International Version)

- **1 Cor 5:17-19**

  17 Therefore, if anyone is in Christ, he is a new creation; the old has gone, the new has come! 18 All this is from God, who reconciled us to himself through Christ and gave us the ministry of reconciliation: 19 that God was reconciling the world to himself in Christ, not counting men's sins against them.

  (New International Version)

Important things to look for as you grow in things of God and his reality begins to manifest in your reality:

- First, align your thoughts with what God says about you instead of what the world says about you.

  o 1 Cor 2:12-15

  12 We have not received the spirit of the world but the Spirit who is from God, that we may understand what God has freely given us. 13 This is what we speak, not in words taught us by human wisdom but in words taught by the Spirit, expressing spiritual truths in spiritual words. 14 The man without the Spirit does not accept the things that come from the Spirit of God, for they are foolishness to him, and he cannot understand them, because they are spiritually discerned. 15 The spiritual man makes judgments about all things, but he himself is not subject to any man's judgment.

  (New International Version)

- Allow your thoughts to be less and less dictated by what you see and do.

    - 2 Cor 5:7
      For we walk by faith, not by sight
      (American Standard Version)

    - Col 1:13-14
      13 For he has rescued us from the dominion of darkness and brought us into the kingdom of the Son he loves, 14 in whom we have redemption, the forgiveness of sins.
      (New International Version)

- Allow your thoughts to be dictated more and more by God's truth about who you are in Christ Jesus.

    - Rom 8:1-11
      Therefore, there is now no condemnation for those who are in Christ Jesus, 2 because through Christ Jesus the law of the Spirit of life set me free from the law of sin and death. 3 For what the law was powerless to do in that it was weakened by the sinful nature, God did by sending his own Son in the likeness of sinful man to be a sin offering. And so he condemned sin in sinful man, 4 in order that the

righteous requirements of the law might be fully met in us, who do not live according to the sinful nature but according to the Spirit. 5 Those who live according to the sinful nature have their minds set on what that nature desires; but those who live in accordance with the Spirit have their minds set on what the Spirit desires. 6 The mind of sinful man is death, but the mind controlled by the Spirit is life and peace; 7 the sinful mind is hostile to God. It does not submit to God's law, nor can it do so. 8 Those controlled by the sinful nature cannot please God. 9 You, however, are controlled not by the sinful nature but by the Spirit, if the Spirit of God lives in you. And if anyone does not have the Spirit of Christ, he does not belong to Christ. 10 But if Christ is in you, your body is dead because of sin, yet your spirit is alive because of righteousness. 11 And if the Spirit of him who raised Jesus from the dead is living in you, he who raised Christ from the dead will also give life to your mortal bodies through his Spirit, who lives in you.

(New International Version)

- Second, allow the words coming out of your mouth to be aligned with God's spiritual truth about who you are, and less aligned with what you see in the world.

- This is critical. Be aware of the words you say. Words are either life or death.

    - Proverbs 18:21
      The tongue has the power of life and death,
      and those who love it will eat its fruit.
      (New International Version)

    - Deuteronomy 8:3
      He humbled you, causing you to hunger and then feeding you with manna, which neither you nor your fathers had known, to teach you that man does not live on bread alone but on every word that comes from the mouth of the LORD.
      (New International Version)

- Finally, God's truth begins to shape your natural world instead of what you see in the world that shapes your thoughts and beliefs.

    - When your world does not line up with God's truth, you must stay faithful to God's Word.

        - Heb 11:1-3
          To have faith is to be sure of the things we hope for, to be certain of the things we cannot see. 2 It was by their faith that people of ancient times won God's

approval. 3 It is by faith that we understand that the universe was created by God's word, so that what can be seen was made out of what cannot be seen.

(TEV)

- Only then does God's truth begin to manifest itself in your physical world.
- That manifestation forces your world to align with God's truth, the only truth.

- The world's deception no longer has power over your life.

  - 1 John 5:5
    Who is it that overcomes the world? Only he who believes that Jesus is the Son of God.
    (New International Version)

- You are truth: talking truth, walking truth, being truth effortlessly.

  - 2 Cor 5:7
    For we walk by faith, not by sight
    (American Standard Version)

- o 2 Corinthians 5:17
  Therefore, if anyone is in Christ, he is a new creation; the old has gone, the new has come!
  (New International Version)

Hear Christ + Think Christ + Know Christ + Believe Christ + Speak Christ = Be Christ-like

<u>The Life of Christ:</u>

- **Romans 8:2-4**
  Therefore, there is now no condemnation for those who are in Christ Jesus, 2 because through Christ Jesus the law of the Spirit of life set me free from the law of sin and death. 3 For what the law was powerless to do in that it was weakened by the sinful nature, God did by sending his own Son in the likeness of sinful man to be a sin offering. And so he condemned sin in sinful man, 4 in order that the righteous requirements of the law might be fully met in us, who do not live according to the sinful nature but according to the Spirit.
  (New International Version)

- Can you give me examples of God's spirit realm manifesting itself in the physical world whereby aligning the world to God's truth?

- That's easy. Read the life of Jesus, and you will be amazed how the physical world was turned upside down by God's spiritual reality.
  - The blind could see.
  - The lame could walk.
  - The sick, healed.
  - The dead, raised.
  - The bound, delivered.
  - The impossible became possible.

  - Matt 11:5-6

    5 "The blind receive sight, the lame walk, those who have leprosy are cured, the deaf hear, the dead are raised, and the good news is preached to the poor. 6 Blessed is the man who does not fall away on account of me."

    (New International Version)

- So when you read the life of Christ, understand what you're reading. It is God's truth in the spirit realm revealing itself in the physical world.

- Christ was not moved by what he saw in the world but by the Spirit, his Father. Jesus only spoke what his Father told him to speak. Jesus only did what his Father told him to do.

- 2 Corinthians 5:7
  We walk by faith, not by sight.
  (New International Version)

- The previous examples are what it looks like when God's truth, His Word, is manifested in the world in which we live: The natural world aligning to God's spiritual world.

- Remember, these things will happen in your life, too, according to Word of God.

- It all starts by feeding your spirit with God's truth.

- People like to call them miracles, but in reality, is the natural world coming in line with God's spiritual truth.

Hear Truth + Think Truth + Know Truth + Believe Truth + Speak Truth = Be Truth

Feeding Your Spirit Man:

- How do you feed your spirit?

- Start by hearing the word of God.

- Rom 10:17

  So then faith cometh by hearing, and hearing by the word of God.

  (King James Version)

- Luke 4:20-21

  20 Then he rolled up the scroll, gave it back to the attendant and sat down. The eyes of everyone in the synagogue were fastened on him, 21 and he began by saying to them, "Today this scripture is fulfilled in your hearing."

  (New International Version)

- Gal 3:5

  He therefore that ministereth to you the Spirit, and worketh miracles among you, doeth he it by the works of the law, or by the hearing of faith?

  (King James Version)

- Heb 11:1-3

  To have faith (in the Grace of our Father) is to be sure of the things we hope for, to be certain of the things we cannot see. 2 It was by their faith (in the Grace of God) that people of ancient times won God's approval. 3 It is by faith (in Grace of God) that we understand that the universe was created by God's word, so that what can be seen was made out of what cannot be seen.

  (TEV)

- As you meditate on God's word, it is important to keep it in a spiritual context.
- For example, when reading about who you are in Christ Jesus, that is you, your spirit man, in the Spirit of Christ, which is spiritual material all based on faith, this is the only way you can read about spiritual things and accept them as truths for your life.
- Anything that does not align with who God says you are is a lie. Don't buy what they're selling. Walk by faith, not by sight!
- When reading about the miracles of Jesus Christ, remember this is God's truth manifesting into the physical world.

- These are things that will happen as you grow in the spirit.

    - Matt 11:5-6
      5 The blind receive sight, the lame walk, those who have leprosy are cured, the deaf hear, the dead are raised, and the good news is preached to the poor. 6 Blessed is the man who does not fall away on account of me."

      (New International Version)

- Don't take my word for it; take God's Word because He said it.

    - John 14:12
      12 I tell you the truth, anyone who has faith in me (my Grace for you) will do what I have been doing. He will do even greater things than these, because I am going to the Father.
      (New International Version)

- That means: it must be true.
- That means: it is a reality in the spirit realm/world.
- That means: anything I see or hear that is contrary to God's Word is a lie.
- That means: I choose to believe the truth and not the lie, regardless of what I see or what I feel.
- That means: I will think the Word; I will know the Word; I will believe the Word; I will speak the Word, regardless of what I see and how I feel in the world.
- That means God's truth will manifest in my physical world because God's spiritual truths always take precedent over the natural world.

    - Heb 11:3
      It is by faith that we understand that the universe was created by God's word, so that what can be seen was made out of what cannot be seen.
      (TEV)

- Col 1:15-16

  15 He is the image of the invisible God, the firstborn over all creation. 16 For by him all things were created: things in heaven and on earth, visible and invisible, whether thrones or powers or rulers or authorities; all things were created by him and for him.

  (New International Version)

- God's children who know who they are in Christ Jesus and walk by faith in the Grace of our Father and not by sight will be the truth. They will think truth, talk truth, walk truth, and live truth effortlessly.

  - John 14:12-21

    12 I tell you the truth, anyone who has faith in me (in my Grace for you) will do what I have been doing. He will do even greater things than these, because I am going to the Father. 13 And I will do whatever you ask in my name, so that the Son may bring glory to the Father. 14 You may ask me for anything in my name, and I will do it. 15 "If you love me, you will obey what I command (to Have Faith in my Mercy and Goodness). 16 And I will ask the Father, and he will give you another Counselor to be with you forever- 17 the Spirit of truth. The world cannot accept him, because it neither sees him nor knows him. But you know him, for he lives with you and will be in you. 18 I will not leave you as orphans; I will come to you. 19 Before long, the world will not see me anymore, but you will see me. Because I live, you also will live. 20 On that day you will realize that I am in my Father, and you are in me, and I am in you. 21 Whoever has my commands (Loves and has Faith in my Mercy and Goodness) and obeys them, he is the one who loves me. He who loves me will be loved by my Father, and I too will love him and show myself to him."

(New International Version)

Hear Christ + Think Christ + Know Christ + Believe Christ + Speak Christ = Be Christ-like

Give You Specific Instruction to Overcome Those Obstacles and Avoid the Pitfalls that Exists in This World

It is critical to overcome the obstacles and avoid pitfalls as you begin your journey to start living God's purpose for your life today. Remember, before you can see miracles like the ones Jesus performed, and the ones God says you too will experience, a spiritual process must occur. This journey requires dedication and commitment to God's Word, but the rewards are great and eternal. There is no question that the treasure you uncover for your life as you begin this journey will be more precious than silver and gold. There are several levels and key issues for which to watch as you grow in the things of the Spirit.

Your Journey Begins Today:

- **1st level** – The early manifestation of the spirit world making its way into your physical world will start by recognizing when things are contrary to the Word of God. That starts with knowing the Word of God. Know His mercy and goodness by reading God's Word.

- **2nd level** – You'll begin to make a conscious choice either accept what you see in the world or believe in what God says. It is your choice, and only you can make it. Before this journey, you accepted the reality of the world and never questioned it; now, for the first time in your life, you know there is an alternative to what you see in the world. I'm not suggesting you won't struggle in these early stages between believing what you see and hear in the world, and what the Word of God says to be so. After all, this is how we have lived our entire lives. Our belief systems do not change overnight. It takes faith. But the difference now is you are aware that there is a choice before you, one you never knew was there before. This may sound impossible to do, but not with God, with whom all things are possible!

- **3rd level** – You will know serious progress has been made when your thoughts begin aligning with God's truth. You start believing God's Word over your life despite your circumstances!

    - Heb 11:1-4
      Now faith is the assurance of things hoped for, the conviction of things not seen. 2 For by it the men of old gained approval. 3 By faith we understand that the worlds were prepared by the word of God, so that what is seen was not made out of things which are visible.

      (NASU)

- **4th level** - Your words start aligning with God's Word and not agreeing with what the physical world projects. You begin to realize that words are powerful and they recreate and create. God created the universe by speaking it into existence: a great example of the spirit taking precedence. You, just like God, have the power to speak those things into existence, good or bad.

    - Heb 11:3
      It is by faith that we understand that the universe was created by God's word, so that what can be seen was made out of what cannot be seen.

      (TEV)

- Gen 1:4

  In the beginning God created the heavens and the earth. 2 Now the earth was formless and empty, darkness was over the surface of the deep, and the Spirit of God was hovering over the waters.3 And God said, "Let there be light," and there was light. 4 God saw that the light was good, and he separated the light from the darkness.

  (New International Version)

- Heb 4:12

  For the word of God is living, and active, and sharper than any two-edged sword, and piercing even to the dividing of soul and spirit, of both joints and marrow, and quick to discern the thoughts and intents of the heart.

  (ASV)

- Rom 6:22-23

  22 But now that you have been set free from sin and have become slaves to God, the benefit you reap leads to holiness, and the result is eternal life. 23 For the wages of sin is death, but the gift of God is eternal life in Christ Jesus our Lord.

  (New International Version)

- **5th level** – Your reality is no longer affected by the reality of the world, just like God. Deception no longer has power over your life!

    - Luke 17:6
    He replied, "If you have faith as small as a mustard seed, you can say to this mulberry tree, 'Be uprooted and planted in the sea,' and it will obey you."
    (New International Version)

    - John 14:12-14
    12 I tell you the truth, anyone who has faith in me will do what I have been doing. He will do even greater things than these, because I am going to the Father. 13 And I will do whatever you ask in my name, so that the Son may bring glory to the Father. 14 You may ask me for anything in my name, and I will do it.
    (New International Version)

    - 1 John 4:16-17
    We have come to know and have believed the love which God has for us. God is love, and the one who abides in love abides in God, and God abides in him. 17 By this, love is perfected with us, so that we may have confidence in the day of judgment; because as He is [right NOW], so also are we in this world.

- Mark 11:23

  I tell you the truth, if anyone says to this mountain, 'Go, throw yourself into the sea,' and does not doubt in his heart but believes that what he says will happen, it will be done for him.

  (New International Version)

- **The Breakthrough level** – I like to call this the Matrix Moment. In the movie, *The Matrix*, Neo finally breaks through the matrix and sees the deception with his spiritual eyes.

- No more fear and anxiety, only peace and joy because the truth did set him free and can set us free too!

- That is what I call being truth: thinking truth, talking truth, walking truth, and living truth effortlessly.

  - Luke 4:18-21

    18 "The Spirit of the Lord is on me,
    because he has anointed me to preach good news to the poor.
    He has sent me to proclaim freedom for the prisoners and recovery of sight for the blind, to release the oppressed,

19 to proclaim the year of the Lord's favor." 20 Then he rolled up the scroll, gave it back to the attendant and sat down. The eyes of everyone in the synagogue were fastened on him, 21 and he began by saying to them, "Today this scripture is fulfilled in your hearing."

(New International Version)

o John 14:9-21

9 Jesus answered: "Don't you know me, Philip, even after I have been among you such a long time? Anyone who has seen me has seen the Father. How can you say, 'Show us the Father'? 10 Don't you believe that I am in the Father, and that the Father is in me? The words I say to you are not just my own. Rather, it is the Father, living in me, who is doing his work. 11 Believe me when I say that I am in the Father and the Father is in me; or at least believe on the evidence of the miracles themselves. 12 I tell you the truth, anyone who has faith in me will do what I have been doing. He will do even greater things than these, because I am going to the Father. 13 And I will do whatever you ask in my name, so that the Son may bring glory to the Father. 14 You may ask me for anything in my name, and I will do it. 15 If you love me, you will obey what I command. 16 And I will ask the Father, and he will give you another Counselor to be with you forever- 17 the Spirit of truth. The world cannot accept him, because it neither sees him nor knows him. But you know him, for he lives with you and will be in you. 18 I will not leave you as orphans; I will come to you. 19 Before long, the world will not see me anymore, but you will see me. Because I live, you also will live. 20 On that day you will realize that I am in my Father, and you are in me, and I am in you. 21 Whoever has my commands and obeys them, he is the one who loves me. He who loves me will be loved by my Father, and I too will love him and show myself to him."

(New International Version)

Hear Truth + Know Truth + Think Truth + Believe Truth + Speak Truth = Be Truth

Reveal How You Will Operate in the World as You Be the Truth and How Your World Will Look and Respond as You Do

Everything begins with faith. It takes faith to believe in God. It certainly takes faith to believe what God says about you and me. Especially when the things we see around us, with our very own eyes, contradict what God says about the situation. It all starts with faith, so we must build up our faith. According to the Bible, we can do this by hearing the Word of God again and again and again. Faith comes by hearing and hearing by the Word of God.

- Rom 10:17
  So then faith cometh by hearing, and hearing by the word of God.
  (King James Version)

- Luke 17:6
  He replied, "If you have faith as small as a mustard seed, you can say to this mulberry tree, 'Be uprooted and planted in the sea,' and it will obey you."
  (New International Version)

- Luke 7:9-10
  9 When Jesus heard this, he was amazed at him, and turning to the crowd following him, he said, "I tell you, I have not found such great faith even in Israel." 10 Then the men who had been sent returned to the house and found the servant well.
  (New International Version)

- Mark 11:23
  I tell you the truth, if anyone says to this mountain, 'Go, throw yourself into the sea,' and does not doubt in his heart but believes that what he says will happen, it will be done for him.
  (New International Version)

The Power of Faith:

- Read about the life of Jesus. As you read, keep in mind that Jesus' life was all about walking in the spirit. Jesus was led by the Spirit. So when reading about the life of Christ, you get a fantastic perspective on what it's like to live as a new creation on this earth: what it truly means to walk by faith and not by sight.

- Imagine living that life today, right now. After all, God gave his only begotten son so that we no longer have to live under the law of sin and death but in power and glory.

- Imagine a day where you have no anxiety because all is right in the spirit world, based on God's Word, God's truth, and you know it to be so, regardless of what you see in the natural realm.

- Your spirit world, free from sin and death, is aligned with your physical world and manifested in your physical world. This makes for a pretty awesome place to be, just like God your Father intended it to be for you and me in the first place.

    - Rom 8:1-4
      8:1 Therefore, there is now no condemnation for those who are in Christ Jesus, 2 because through Christ Jesus the law of the Spirit of life set me free from the law of sin and death. 3 For what the law was powerless to do in that it was weakened by the sinful nature, God did by sending his own Son in the likeness of sinful

man to be a sin offering. And so he condemned sin in sinful man, 4 in order that the righteous requirements of the law might be fully met in us, who do not live according to the sinful nature but according to the Spirit.

(New International Version)

- In the spirit world, sin and death have no power over your life. Therefore, there is no sickness, disease, addictions, anxiety, depression, rejection, or anything evil the enemy may have convinced you of otherwise.

  - Isaiah 53:5
    But he was pierced for our transgressions, he was crushed for our iniquities; the punishment that brought us peace was upon him, and by his wounds we are healed.

    (New International Version)

  - I Peter 2:24
    He personally carried our sins in his body on the cross so that we can be dead to sin and live for what is right. By his wounds you are healed.

    (New Living Translation)

- You are living truth, the truth that God has spoken over your life.

2 Cor 5:17-21

17 Therefore, if anyone is in Christ, he is a new creation; the old has gone, the new has come! 18 All this is from God, who reconciled us to himself through Christ and gave us the ministry of reconciliation: 19 that God was reconciling the world to himself in Christ, not counting men's sins against them. And he has committed to us the message of reconciliation. 20 We are therefore Christ's ambassadors, as though God were making his appeal through us. We implore you on Christ's behalf: Be reconciled to God. 21 God made him who had no sin to be sin for us, so that in him we might become the righteousness of God.

(New International Version)

Hear Christ + Think Christ + Know Christ + Believe Christ + Speak Christ = Be Christ-like

The Good News:

- **Mark 16:15**

  He said to them, "Go into all the world and preach the good news to all creation."

  (New International Version)

- **John 17:20-26**
  20"My prayer is not for them alone. I pray also for those who will believe in me through their message, 21that all of them may be one, Father, just as you are in me and I am in you. May they also be in us so that the world may believe that you have sent me. 22I have given them the glory that you gave me, that they may be one as we are one: 23I in them and you in me. May they be brought to complete unity to let the world know that you sent me and have loved them even as you have loved me. 24"Father, I want those you have given me to be with me where I am, and to see my glory, the glory you have given me because you loved me before the creation of the world. 25"Righteous Father, though the world does not know you, I know you, and they know that you have sent me. 26I have made you known to them, and will continue to make you known in order that the love you have for me may be in them and that I myself may be in them"
  (New International Version)

- It is your choice because God has already chosen you.

  o 2 Thessalonians 2:13
  But we ought always to thank God for you, brothers loved by the Lord, because from the beginning God chose you to be saved through the sanctifying work of the Spirit and through belief in the truth.

(New International Version)

- Imagine the possibilities as nothing is impossible through Christ Jesus.

    - Mark 10:27
      Jesus looked at them and said, "With man this is impossible, but not with God; all things are possible with God."
      (New International Version)

- Practice makes perfect. I suggest every morning, when you wake up, pray and seek God's direction. Invite the Holy Spirit into all that you do: every action, word, or step in line with God's perfect will, and it will bring glory to our Father God.

- The steps of a good man are ordered by the Lord. That is the way you should start thinking about living your spiritual life as a spirit being. Your steps have been ordered by the Lord!

    - Psalms 37:23
      The steps of a good man are ordered by the LORD: and he delighteth in his way.
      (New International Version)

- That is exactly how Jesus lived his life: every day, he knew everything he did was in the perfect will of God, right down to healing the sick and raising the dead. Jesus truly lived God's purpose for his life every day, and you can, too!

    - John 15:10
      "And He who sent Me is with Me; He has not left Me alone, for I always do the things that are pleasing to Him."

      (New International Version)

- Imagine what it would be like to live as Jesus did by just being. All I know is it would be beyond amazing: God's will on earth as it is in heaven.

- Imagine the conversations Jesus had with our Father God, Moses, Elijah, and Abraham, pretty amazing stuff! Should we expect anything less? We do serve an amazing God!

    - Mark 9:4
      And there appeared before them Elijah and Moses, who were talking with Jesus.

      (New International Version)

- That is the world in which Jesus lived, and this is the world God wants for you.

    - John 14:12-14
    12 I tell you the truth, anyone who has faith in me will do what I have been doing. He will do even greater things than these, because I am going to the Father. 13 And I will do whatever you ask in my name, so that the Son may bring glory to the Father. 14 You may ask me for anything in my name, and I will do it.
    (New International Version)

    - John 1:50-51
    Jesus said, "You believe because I told you I saw you under the fig tree. You shall see greater things than that." 51 He then added, "I tell you the truth, you shall see heaven open, and the angels of God ascending and descending on the Son of Man."
    (New International Version)

    - Matthew 11:5
    The blind receive sight, the lame walk, those who have leprosy are cured, the deaf hear, the dead are raised, and the good news is preached to the poor.
    (New International Version)

- Matthew 17:20
  He replied, "Because you have so little faith. I tell you the truth, if you have faith as small as a mustard seed, you can say to this mountain, 'Move from here to there' and it will move. Nothing will be impossible for you."
  (New International Version)

- God's work is perfected in the death of Jesus. He gave His only begotten son to redeem the world and break the chains of sin and death over our lives to restore us under the blessings of Abraham.

- Now it is up to you to take the last step by doing the following:

- Know who God says you are in Christ Jesus. "My people are destroyed for lack of knowledge" (Hosea 4:6).

- You have the power to choose life: you do this by choosing to believe who God says you are and not what you see, hear, or do in the world.

  - Deut 30:19
    This day I call heaven and earth as witnesses against you that I have set before you life and death, bless-

ings and curses. Now choose life, so that you and your children may live.

(New International Version)

- Go daily before the cross. Remember His blood, His grace, His gift, His righteousness which is your righteousness. Jesus is not talking about you going before the cross talking about how worthless you are or that you don't deserve any of it. It's not about you. Deny yourself. Thank your Father for forgiving your sins, past, present, and future, and walk in that same forgiveness that Christ afforded you. Be as our Father is according to the eternal Word of God: this is critical. Confess God's Word over your life daily. Speak to your spirit, mind, and body about who God says you are.

    - Luke 9:23

      Then he said to them all: "If anyone would come after me, he must deny himself and take up his cross daily and follow me."

      (New International Version)

    - 1 John 4:16-17

      We have come to know and have believed the love which God has for us. God is love, and the one who abides in love abides in God, and God abides in him.

17 By this, love is perfected with us, so that we may have confidence in the day of judgment; because as He is [right NOW], so also are we in this world.

- Believe God's word about you regardless of how you're behaving at the time or the feedback you are getting from the world. He that is in you is greater than he that is in the world.

    - I John 4:4
      You, dear children, are from God and have overcome them, because the one who is in you is greater than the one who is in the world.
      (New International Version)

- With God, failure is impossible.

    - Mark 10:27
      Jesus looked at them and said, "With man this is impossible, but not with God; all things are possible with God."
      (New International Version)

- That is an amazing thing to write and it is the truth!

Hear Truth + Know Truth + Think Truth + Believe Truth + Speak Truth = Be Truth

Give You a Practical Guide On How to Get Started Today

For the blessings of the Lord await you. Today is the day the Lord has made; rejoice and glad in it.

Starting your journey today:

- Let's start with technology. Use it for good!
- Did you know most streaming services have the Bible for free to download and listen to on a continuous loop?
- Listen to the Bible every chance you have, as technology makes it so easy to do so.
- Technology allows us to hear God's Word without really changing anything we do. Let technology start working for us in building the kingdom of God.
- Remember: Faith comes by hearing, and hearing by the Word of God.

- It truly takes unwavering faith to believe God's Word about who we are, based on the blood of Jesus, because our actions are often not very godly. As you know by now, our righteousness is not qualified or disqualified by our performance.
- God is the author and finisher of my faith! Do your part: hearing, hearing, and hearing God's Word. He will do the rest.
- Thank God for Jesus Christ and the life-saving and merciful blood he shed for all our sins.
- You are solely responsible for feeding your spirit with the word of God.
- Remember that your human ears are the mouth of your spirit.
- So feed your spirit by hearing the Word of God as much as you can.
- God will take it from there. Trust God to reveal himself to you.

Hear God's Word + Think God's Word + Know God's Word + Believe God's Word + Speak God's Word = Be God's Word

Hear Truth + Know Truth + Think Truth + Believe Truth + Speak Truth = Be Truth

Hear Christ + Think Christ + Know Christ + Believe Christ + Speak Christ = Be Christ-like

Recap: How to Live God's Purpose for Your Life Today

- **Establish basic truths about the Word of God.**
  - God's Word has the final say so.

- **Reveal God's purpose for your life on this earth.**
  - Be truth
    - Love God with all your heart
    - Love your neighbor as you love yourself

- **Reveal who you are according to God, your Creator.**
  - Who God is, so are you through his mercy and grace.

- **Examine the pitfalls that prevent you from living God's purpose on this earth.**
  - Choosing not to believe in God's Word because of what you see in the world.

- **Give you specific instruction to overcome those obstacles and avoid the pitfalls that exist in this world.**
    - Believe God's Word no matter what.

- **Reveal how you will operate in the world as you be truth and how your world will look and respond as you do.**
    - Peace and joy will come upon you, and signs and wonders will follow you.

- **Give you a practical guide on how to get started today.**
    - Hear God's Word + Think God's Word + Know God's Word + Believe God's Word + Speak God's Word = Be God's Word

My prayer for you:

I pray that God may reveal himself to you every day and that you walk in the purpose, power, and glory of our Savior, Christ Jesus!

Final words:

Just be. Rest in the finished work of Jesus Christ as He is the great I Am. Everything you lack He is for you.

He is your redeemer, your righteousness, your healer, your provider, your protector, your strength, your everything! You and you alone have the amazing power to choose what God your Creator says about you! By all means, choose life!

John 3:17

For **God** did **not** send **His Son** into the world to **condemn** the **world**, but that the world through **Him** might be **saved.**

(New King James Version)

John 19:30

So when **Jesus** had received the sour wine, He said, **"It is finished!"** And bowing His head, He gave up His spirit.

(New King James Version)

Romans 8:39

nor **height** nor **depth**, nor any other **created thing**, shall be able to **separate us** from the **love** of **God** which is in **Christ Jesus our Lord**.

(New King James Version)

2 Corinthians 5:17

Therefore, if **anyone** is in **Christ**, he is a **new creation**; old things have passed away; behold, all things have become **new**.

(New King James Version)

1 John 4:17

Love has been perfected among us in this: that we may have boldness in the day of judgment; because as **He is, so are we in this world**

(New King James Version)

Hear Christ + Think Christ + Know Christ + Believe Christ + Speak Christ = Be Christ-like

CPSIA information can be obtained
at www.ICGtesting.com
Printed in the USA
LVHW010800130821
694825LV00007B/99

9 781637 692141